Insects

KINGFISHER

LONDON & NEW YORK

First published as *Kingfisher Young Knowledge: Insects* in 2006
Additional material produced for Kingfisher by Discovery Books Ltd.

Distributed in the U.S. by Macmillan, 175 Fifth Ave., New York, NY 10010
Distributed in Canada by H.B. Fenn and Company Ltd.,
34 Nixon Road, Bolton, Ontario L7E 1W2

Library of Congress Cataloging-in-Publication data has been applied for.

ISBN: 978-0-7534-6449-6

Kingfisher books are available for special promotions and premiums.
For details contact: Special Markets Department, Macmillan,
175 Fifth Avenue, New York, NY 10010.

For more information, please visit www.kingfisherbooks.com

Printed in China
10 9 8 7 6 5 4 3 2 1

1TR/0410/WKT/UNTD/140MA/C

Note to readers: the website addresses listed in this book are correct at
the time of going to print. However, due to the ever-changing nature
of the Internet, website addresses and content can change. Websites
can contain links that are unsuitable for children. The publisher cannot
be held responsible for changes in website addresses or content or
for information obtained through a third party. We strongly advise
that Internet searches be supervised by an adult.

Acknowledgments

The publishers would like to thank the following for permission to reproduce their material. Every care has been taken
to trace copyright holders. However, if there have been unintentional omissions or failure to trace copyright holders,
we apologize and will, if informed, endeavor to make corrections in any future edition.
b = bottom, *c* = center, *l* = left, *t* = top, *r* = right

Cover main Shutterstock/Gallofoto; cover *l* Shutterstock/Kletr; cover *r* Shutterstock/Arvind Balaraman; 1 Frank Lane Picture Agency (FLPA)/Michael & Patricia Fogden;
2-3 Nature Picture Library (Naturepl)/Ingo Arndt; 4–5 Corbis/Michael & Patricia Fogden; 6–7 FLPA/Minden; 7*tr* FLPA/Panda Photo; 7*br* Getty Dorling Kindersley;
8*l* FLPA/Foto Natura; 8–9 FLAP/Roger Wilmshurst; 9*r* FLPA/B. Borrell Casals; 10*b* Ardea/Pascal Goetgheluck; 10–11 FLPA/Minden; 11*tr* Ardea/Steve Hopkin;
12 FLPA/Minden; 12–13 Naturepl/Ingo Arndt; 13*tr* Natural History Picture Agency (NHPA)/ Stephen Dalton; 14*cr* NHPA/James Carmichael; 14*cl* FLPA/
Foto Natura; 14*bl* Naturepl/Duncan McEwan; 15 Photolibrary.com; 16 NHPA/Paal Hermansen; 17*t* Ardea/Steve Hopkin; 17*b* FLPA/Minden; 18 Photolibary.com;
19*t* Photolibrary.com; 19*b* FLPA/Derek Middleton; 20*bl* Naturepl/Premaphotos; 21*tr* FLPA/Richard Becker; 21*b* FLPA/Foto Natura; 22*lc* Science Photo Library (SPL)/
Susumu Nishinaga; 22*bl* Naturepl/Warwick Sloss; 23*t* Ardea/Steve Hopkin; 23*cl* SPL/Nuridsany & Perennou; 23*cr* SPL/Susumu Nishinaga; 23*br* Naturepl/
Ross Hoddinott; 24–25 Naturepl/Premaphotos; 24*b* FLPA/Foto Natura; 25*br* Ardea/John Mason; 26 Corbis/Anthony Bannister; 26*bl* FLPA/Foto Natura;
27*b* Naturepl/Martin Dohrn; 28*cl* Alamy; 28*br* Photolibrary.com; 29 Naturepl/Michael Durham; 29*b* Getty NGS; 30 Corbis/Anthony Bannister; 31*t* NHPA/George
Bernard; 31*b* FLPA/Foto Natura; 32 FLPA/Minden 33*tr* FLPA/Derek Middleton; 33*b* FLPA/Minden; 34–35 Photolibrary.com; 34*b* Photolibrary.com; 35*tr* Photolibrary.com;
36 Photolibrary.com; 37*t* Naturepl/Martin Dohrn; Corbis/Anthony Bannister; 38 Alamy/Peter Arnold Inc.; 39*t* Alamy/Robert Pickett; 39*b* Alamy/Maximilian Weinzierl;
48*t* Shutterstock Images/Yaroslav; 48*b* Shutterstock Images/Christian Musat; 49*t* Shutterstock Images/Jamie Wilson; 49*c* Shutterstock Images/Le Do; 52*t* Shutterstock
Images/Yellowj; 52*b* Shutterstock Images/M. Dykstra; 53*t* Shutterstock Images/Dark Raptor; 53*b* Shutterstock Images/Javarman; 56*t* Shutterstock Images/Zvenis

Commissioned photography on pages 42–47 by Andy Crawford
Thank you to models Alex Bandy, Alastair Carter, Tyler Gunning, and Lauren Signist

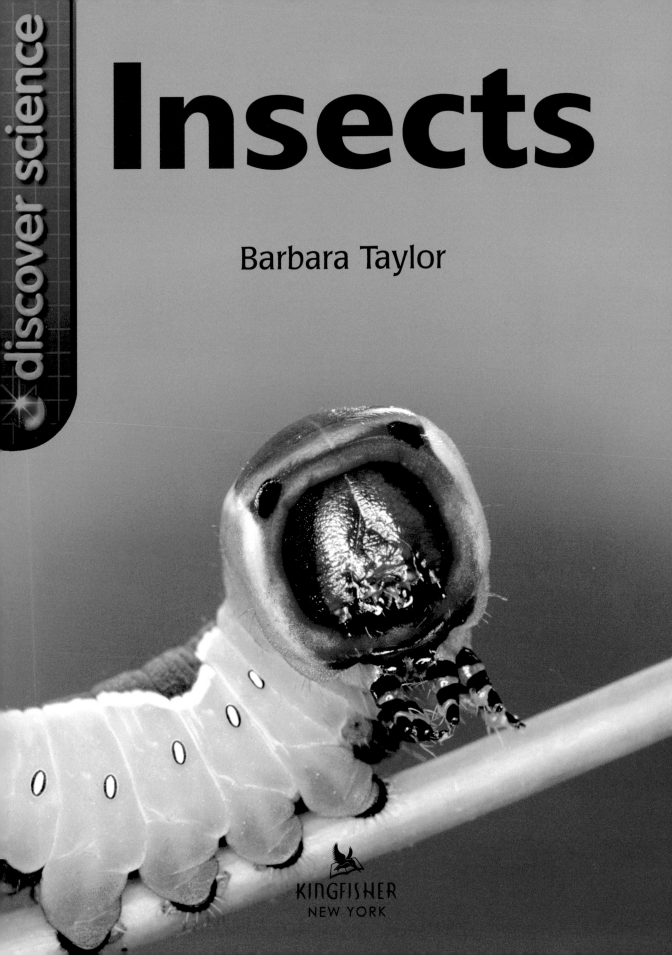

discover science

Insects

Barbara Taylor

KINGFISHER
NEW YORK

Contents

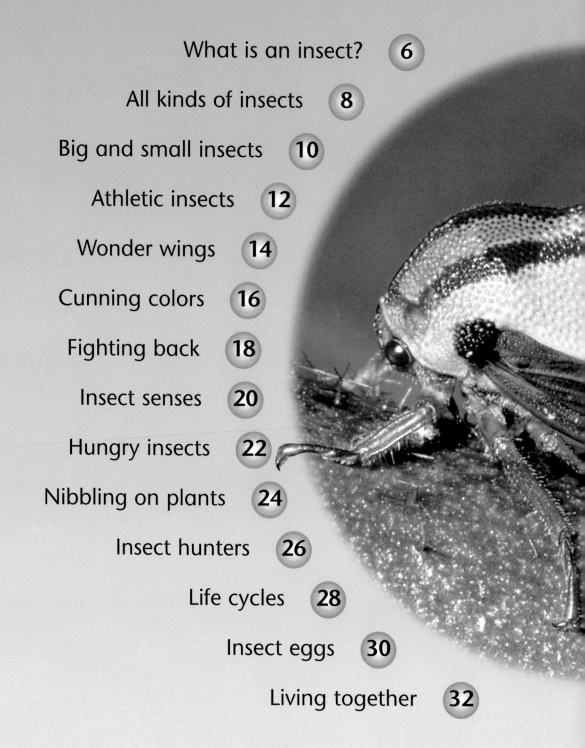

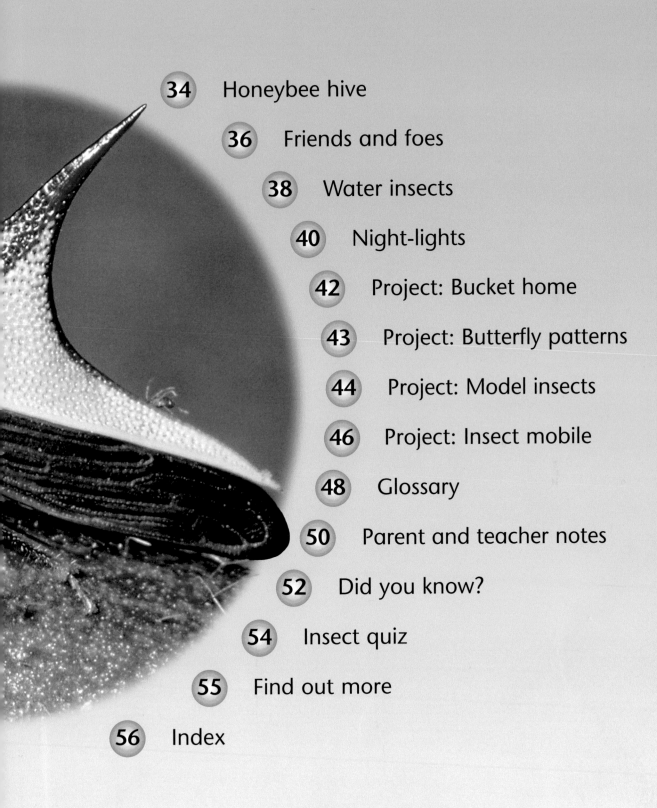

What is an insect?

An insect is a small animal with six legs and three sections to its body. A hard outer skeleton covers and protects an insect's body like a suit of armor.

dragonfly

Wonderful wings

Most insects have one or two pairs of wings. Their wings are thin flaps that are made from the outer body covering. The wings are connected to the thorax, the middle part of an insect's body.

Early insects

The first insects lived on Earth more than 400 million years ago—long before people were around. This insect was trapped in the sticky sap that oozed from a tree and was preserved for millions of years.

Not an insect!

Spiders, such as this one, are not insects. Spiders have eight legs and only two sections to their body. The head and thorax are joined together. They do not have wings.

All kinds of insects

There are millions of different kinds of insects, which are divided into groups such as beetles, butterflies and moths, bees, wasps, flies, and bugs.

Wasps

Wasps belong to a group of insects that also includes bees and ants. A wasp has a narrow "waist" and folds its wings along the sides of its body.

Flies

A fly has only one pair of wings, but it can fly very well. The fly group includes mosquitoes and bluebottles, like this one.

Butterflies

Butterflies and moths have wings covered in tiny scales that overlap like tiles on a roof. Butterflies, such as this swallowtail, are usually brightly colored and fly during the day.

Big and small insects

Most insects are small creatures—even the biggest ones could fit in your hand. Their small size means that they can live in small spaces and do not need much food.

Tiny fleas

Fleas live among the fur of mammals or the feathers of birds. They have claws to cling on tight and long legs for jumping from one animal to another.

Nasty nits

Head lice thrive in the warmth of human hair, sucking blood from our skin. Female head lice glue their eggs onto the hair. These eggs are known as nits.

Giant wetas

Wetas are giant crickets that live in New Zealand. They probably grew into such huge insects because there were no large mammal predators to eat them.

Athletic insects

Some insects are like human athletes. They are champion sprinters, high jumpers, or weightlifters. Insects use their athletic powers to find food or mates—or even just to stay alive.

Weightlifting
One of these male rhinoceros beetles has managed to lift the other one up off the ground! He has won the chance to mate with the females.

High jump

Insects that are good at high jumping, such as this leafhopper, usually have long back legs powered by strong muscles in the thorax.

Sprinting

Long legs help insects take big strides and sprint (move fast). The legs of this tiger beetle are much longer than its body. At any time, three of its six legs usually touch the ground.

Wonder wings

Insects were the first animals that were able to fly. Flying helps insects find food or mates and to escape danger, but it also uses up a lot of energy.

Long trips

Monarch butterflies fly thousands of miles every year to escape the cold winters of Canada. These long journeys are called migration.

Wing covers

Beetles, such as this ladybug, have two pairs of wings. When a beetle lands, its hard front wings cover and protect its delicate flying wings.

Strong wings

A network of veins in an insect's wings makes them strong and flexible. You can see the veins very clearly on this cicada's wings.

Cunning colors

Dull colors help insects hide from predators. Bright colors or patterns warn predators to stay away because an insect is poisonous or harmful.

Warning colors
The bright red spots on this burnet moth are a warning message that says, "Don't eat me. I contain deadly poison."

Fake wasp

The wasp beetle
cannot sting and
is not dangerous.
Predators leave it
alone because they
think it is a real wasp
that might sting them.

Hide-and-seek

Many insects use
camouflage to hide from
predators by looking like
the plants they live on.
This thorn bug even has a
pretend thorn on its back!

Fighting back

From sharp jaws to painful stingers and chemical weapons, insects have many ways of fighting back when they are attacked by predators.

Ready, aim, fire!

Bombardier beetles spray boiling-hot poison at their enemies. The poison is mixed up inside the beetles' bodies when danger threatens.

Horrible hiss

If these cockroaches are disturbed, they make a loud hissing noise by pushing air out of the breathing holes on their sides. This startles predators, such as spiders, and gives the cockroaches time to escape.

Battling beetle

The devil's coach horse beetle defends itself by curling its abdomen over its back like a scorpion. At the same time, the beetle gives off a terrible smell and snaps its jaws together.

Insect senses

An insect's senses of sight, touch, smell, and hearing are vital to its survival. These senses are often much better than our own, but they work in different ways.

Touch and smell

Insects use their antennae to touch and smell their surroundings. This weevil's antennae have special hairs at the tips to detect smells.

Head fans

When they fly, scarab beetles fan out their antennae to increase their size. This helps the beetles detect any smells.

Eye spy

The big eyes of this fly are made up of thousands of very small eyes. They can see in many different directions at the same time.

Hungry insects

Some insects, such as cockroaches, eat almost anything, but most insects feed on particular kinds of food. Their mouthparts help them hold and chop up solid food or suck up liquid.

Spongy mouth

Flies turn their food into a soupy mush and then use a spongy pad (left) to mop up their meal. They can also taste food with their feet!

Jagged jaws

Insect predators need sharp, spiky jaws for holding and chopping up their prey. Insects that chew plants have blunter jaws to grind and mash up their food.

Drinking straws

Butterflies and moths feed on liquid food such as flower nectar or rotting fruit. They suck up the food through a tube called a proboscis, which works like a straw.

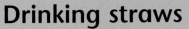

Nibbling on plants

All the different parts of plants are eaten by insects. Some plant-eating insects are farmers, growing their own crops and harvesting seeds.

Leaves for lunch

Leaves do not contain much nutrition, so insects need to eat a lot of them. Grasshoppers are messy eaters, often tearing the leaves as they feed.

Grow-your-own food

Leafcutter ants chew up pieces of leaves and use them to make a mushy compost pile. They grow fungi on the compost, so they always have plenty to eat.

Wood for dinner

Wood contains even less nutrition than leaves, but some insects eat it. Deathwatch beetle larvae spend many years eating damp wood before turning into adults, like this one.

Insect hunters

Insects hunt in three main ways. They may chase after their prey, jump out from a hiding place, or set a trap to catch a meal. Most insects hunt alone, but a few search in groups.

Smart disguise

Many mantises look like leaves. They stay very still and then shoot out their long front legs to grab a passing insect. A mantis has sharp jaws to slice up its prey and scoop out its soft insides.

Soupy snacks

Robber flies catch flying insects with their long, hairy legs. Then they turn the insides of the prey into a liquid soup and suck up their meal.

All together now

Army ants from tropical America hunt in large groups. The ants help one another catch and kill prey. These army ants have caught a centipede.

Life cycles

Many insects have four stages in their life cycle: egg, larva, pupa, and adult. Insect groups that develop this way include beetles, butterflies, moths, flies, fleas, bees, and ants.

1. Egg
A female monarch butterfly lays her eggs underneath the leaves of milkweed plants. Within a week, the eggs hatch into striped caterpillars.

2. Larva
The hungry caterpillar eats and eats and eats. It sheds its skin several times as it grows. This is called molting.

3. Pupa

When the caterpillar is big enough, it turns into a pupa, or chrysalis. Inside its cocoon, the body of the caterpillar changes into the body of a butterfly.

4. Adult

The pupa splits open, and the adult butterfly pulls itself free. It pumps blood into its wings to stretch them out and waits for its wings to dry. Then it flies away to look for a mate.

Insect eggs

Almost all insects start their lives as eggs. The eggs are usually laid on or near food, hidden from predators and bad weather. Very few insects look after their eggs.

Easy meals

Dung beetles shape animal dung into a ball, which they then roll to a safe place. The female lays her eggs inside the dung ball so the young will have food when they hatch.

Caring parent

Female earwigs guard their eggs for months until they hatch. When they do hatch, the babies look like their mother, but without wings.

Male on guard

This male damselfly is holding the female's neck while she lays her eggs on the stems of plants under the water. When the eggs hatch, the young live underwater for the first year.

Living together

Most insects live alone, but a few types live and work together in groups. They are called social insects. All ants and termites—and some bees and wasps—are social insects.

Royal ruler
A big, fat queen termite lays all the eggs in a nest. The smaller worker termites carry her eggs away and bring food to her.

Paper nest

Paper wasps make their
nests by chewing up wood
and mixing it with their
saliva to make wasp
"paper." Inside the nest are
many tiny boxes called cells,
where young wasps can develop.

Special sewing

Weaver ants work together as a team
to make a nest out of leaves that are
glued together with sticky silk. One
ant working on its own would not
be strong enough to do this.

Honeybee hive

People build artificial nests called hives for honeybees. The honeybees make honey from flower nectar mixed with their saliva. Beekeepers take this honey for people to eat.

Wax city

Honeybees use wax made in their bodies to build rows of six-sided boxes called cells. These cells fit tightly together to form a thin sheet called a honeycomb.

Queen bee

The large bee in the middle of this picture is a queen honeybee. She lays all the eggs in a honeybee hive.

Beekeeper

Beekeepers lift the honeycombs out to check on the honey and the baby bees inside. They wear special clothing to protect them from bee stings.

Friends and foes

Many insects are our friends because they help flower seeds develop, and they are an important link in food chains. However, some insects cause problems because they eat crops or carry diseases.

Pollen carriers

Many flowers rely on insects to carry a yellow dust called pollen to other flowers of the same type. Pollen needs to join with the eggs inside flowers before seeds can develop.

Bloodsucker

Female mosquitoes suck blood so that their eggs will develop. Some kinds of mosquitoes pass on diseases, such as malaria and yellow fever, while they feed.

Food chain

From birds and frogs to bears and baby crocodiles, many animals eat insects. They are rich in protein, which is good for making bodies strong.

Water insects

Many insects live in fresh water, where there is plenty of food and protection from predators. Some skate over the surface, some swim, and others lurk at the bottom.

Spare air

Great diving beetles collect air from the surface of the water. They store the air under their wing covers so they can breathe while they are underwater.

Water walker

Water striders can walk on the surface of the water. They have very long legs that spread their weight over a wide area so they do not sink.

Baby dragons

Baby dragonflies live under the water, but the adults live in the air. Baby dragonflies are fierce hunters and eat fish.

Night-lights

Insects glow in the dark to attract mates or prey, warn other insects of danger, or tell predators that they taste bad.

Come and get me

Fireflies and glowworms are beetles that come out at night. Some glow all the time, while others flash their lights on and off in a particular pattern. These light signals are used to attract mates.

Cave curtains

Small flies in New Zealand shine their light down sticky strands hanging from the roofs of caves. Prey insects are attracted to the glowing curtain and become trapped on the strands.

Glowing bugs

A firefly produces a short burst of light when a gas called oxygen mixes with chemicals inside its abdomen. This works in a similar way to the glow-in-the-dark light sticks you see at Halloween.

Bucket home

Bug sleepover

Make a home for the bugs that live near you. Draw pictures of the bugs that crawl inside and write down their names.

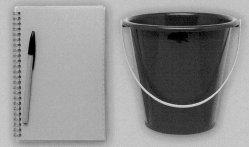

1

You will need:

- Plastic bucket
- Pen and notebook
- Stones, leaves, and grass

Find a damp, shady place near your home. Turn the bucket upside down and balance it on a pile of stones, leaves, and grass. Leave it out overnight and see if any creatures crawl inside.

When you have finished, remember to let the animals go.

Butterfly patterns

Paint a butterfly

The patterns on one wing of a butterfly are the same as on the other side. Paint your own butterfly with matching sides.

You will need
- Heavy paper
- Pencil
- Scissors
- Paints
- Paintbrush
- Pipe cleaners

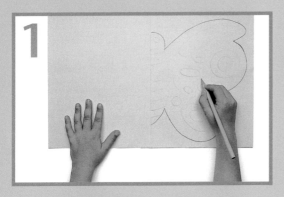

Fold the paper in half and then open it out flat. Use the pencil to draw the outline of half a butterfly on one side of the fold.

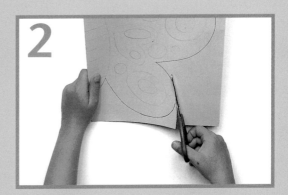

Fold the paper in half again so you can still see your pencil outline. Then carefully cut out the butterfly shape.

Open the paper to see the whole butterfly and use pipe cleaners for its antennae.

Open out the paper and paint one side with thick paints. Then fold your butterfly in half again and press down hard.

Model insects

Make a ladybug

Use papier-mâché to make a model of a giant ladybug. Paint the model red and black, so it looks just like a real ladybug. A ladybug's bright colors warn predators that it is poisonous and tastes bad.

You will need:

- Balloon
- Petroleum jelly
- Paintbrush
- Newspaper
- Flour-and-water paste
- Scissors
- Paints
- Pipe cleaners
- Glue or tape

Ask an adult to help you blow up a balloon. Spread a thick layer of petroleum jelly all over the balloon and then wash your hands.

Cover the whole balloon with strips of newspaper. Brush flour-and-water paste over the newspaper and repeat this about five times.

3

Put the balloon in a warm place to dry. When the surface is hard, use the scissors to carefully cut the model in half.

4

Paint half of the model with ladybug colors. Use pipe cleaners to make the legs and attach them with glue or tape.

Look in books to see if there are any different colored ladybugs and paint the other papier-mâché shape in those colors.

Insect mobile

Make a mobile

Hang this colorful mobile near a window or even outside and watch the insects fly around the flower as the breeze blows.

ladybug

You will need:

- Construction paper (or poster board)
- Pencil
- Paintbrush
- Thin wire
- String
- Tracing paper
- Strong thread
- Apron
- Scissors
- Paints

1

Draw a large flower shape on colored construction paper and cut it out. Paint the flower with colors that you like.

2

Ask an adult to help you make a circle out of wire. Tie four long pieces of string to the wire and knot the ends so the mobile can hang.

Trace or copy the insects on these
pages or draw your own onto
the paper. Cut them out and
paint them to look like insects.

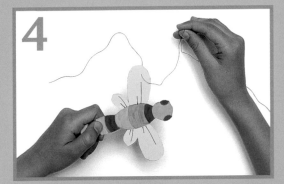

Ask an adult to make small holes
in your flower and insects so you
can tie them to the wire circle.
Your mobile is now ready to hang.

bee

*shield
bug*

dragonfly

Glossary

abdomen—the large part of an insect's body, containing its digestive system

antenna—a long, thin structure on an insect's head used for touching and smelling (plural: antennae)

artificial—human-made

beekeeper—a person who looks after honeybee hives

bug—an insect with sucking mouthparts

camouflage—a shape, color, or pattern that helps an animal hide

compost—a mixture of rotting plants

crop—a plant grown in large amounts to provide food or materials

divided—split into sections

Earth—the planet on which we live

firefly—a glowing beetle that is also called a lightning bug

flexible—able to bend without breaking

foe—an enemy

fungus—a plantlike organism, such as a toadstool, that lives on another organism, either living or dead

glowworm—a female wingless beetle that glows in the dark

harvesting—gathering and storing food

honeycomb—a wax structure made by bees

larva—a young insect that has hatched out of an egg (plural: larvae)

mammal—a hairy animal that feeds its young on mother's milk

mate—to breed or reproduce

migration—the long journey that some animals make to find food or a mate

molting—when an animal molts, it gets rid of its hair or skin

mouthpart—a structure on an insect's head used for feeding

muscle—a part of the body that produces movement

nectar—a sweet liquid made by plants

oxygen—a colorless gas needed by all animals in order to survive

poisonous—describes something that can make you very sick or even kill you if you swallow it

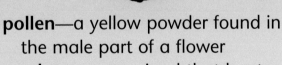

pollen—a yellow powder found in the male part of a flower

predator—an animal that hunts and eats other animals

preserved—protected; kept in its original state

prey—an animal that is killed or eaten by another animal

protein—a substance needed by living things for growth and repair

pupa—a protective case around a developing adult insect

queen—a female that lays the eggs in a group of social insects

sap—a liquid found in the stems and trunks of some plants

skeleton—the structure that supports an animal's body

social—living in a group with others of the same kind, or species

stinger—a sharp needle on an insect's body used for injecting poison

survival—the process of staying alive

termite—a soft-skinned, antlike creature

thorax—the part of an insect's body between its head and abdomen

thrive—to do well

tropical—an area near the equator where it is hot all year long

vein—a narrow tube that carries blood

This book will be useful to help teach and reinforce various elements of the science and language arts curricula. It also provides opportunities for crosscurricular lessons in geography, art, and math.

Extension activities

Language arts:
Writing
1) Choose an interesting insect. Use reference materials to write a report on it. You may wish to follow the model of title, introduction, and three paragraphs of text found on each two-page spread in this book.

2) On pages 18–19 and in several other places, you learned how different insects defend themselves. Imagine a battle between one of these insects and a predator. Write about the incident in one of these styles:
• a newspaper report of the battle
• a diary entry written by the victorious insect
• an eyewitness account written by another insect

Speaking and listening
1) In a short report, describe a day in the life of a particular insect.

2) Create and recite an original poem or song about an insect.

Science
The topic of insects relates to scientific themes of diversity, adaptations, structure and function, growth and development, interdependence, and interaction with the environment. Some specific links to science curriculum content include life cycles (pp. 28–31); food chains and webs (pp. 22–27, 37); behavior (pp. 10–14, 30–35); predator/prey relationships (pp. 11–21, 26–27, 40–41); reproduction (pp. 12, 28–35); and materials (pp. 33–35).

Crosscurricular links
1) *Art and math:* Butterfly wings are symmetrical in color and design. Draw an array of other insects, highlighting their symmetry.

2) *Art and literacy:* Design and create a larger-than-life insect using a variety of materials.

Describe its life story, including its unique characteristics, habitat, behavior, defense mechanisms, place on the food chain, and any special adaptations.

3) *Art:* Design a paper beetle about the size of a quarter. Cut it out and color it so that it can be placed in plain view yet blend in with its surroundings. See if others can spot it.

4) *Geography:* Research the migration of the monarch butterfly. Track the complete journey, listing the states and countries crossed. How is the migration connected to climate?

Using the projects
Children can do these projects at home. Here are some ideas for extending them:

Page 42: Use a hand lens to examine the insects. Set up a small terrarium to observe them over a longer period of time. Keep it damp and provide food. Most ground-dwelling insects will thrive on carrots, squash, or potato slices.

Record daily observations in a science log. Set free anything that isn't eating and thriving.

Pages 44–45: Why stop with a ladybug? Beetles come in all sorts of colors and designs. Use smaller balloons for smaller models.

Page 46–47: Write creative "life stories" about each of the insects on the mobile. Put them together to form a book. Read the stories aloud or act them out.

Did you know?

- Insects are more numerous than all other types of animals in the world put together.

- The noisiest insect in the world is the male cicada, which can be heard from 1,300 feet (400 meters) away.

- The housefly can be dangerous to humans because it carries so many diseases. It also reproduces at a very fast rate. A pair of flies can have an astonishing five billion young a year.

- The human flea can jump 8 inches (20 centimeters) into the air. This is 60 times its body length and the same as a person jumping 360 feet (110 meters)!

- A migrating monarch butterfly once traveled 2,133 miles (3,432 kilometers) from Canada to Mexico. The monarch is the fastest-flying butterfly, clocked at a top speed of 14 miles per hour (22 kilometers per hour).

- At 3.5 ounces (100 grams), the goliath beetle of equatorial Africa is the heaviest insect in the world. This is the same size as a newborn kitten. The male can be more than 4 inches (11 centimeters) long from the tips of its horns to the end of its abdomen.

- Ladybugs won't fly if the temperature is below 55°F (13°C).

- A ladybug's wings are so thin that you can see right through them.

- Imagine being headless! A cockroach can live for an entire week . . . without its head! After being beheaded, the animal can survive for a long time, but there is one problem. Without a head, it has no mouth through which to drink water, so it eventually dies of thirst.

- Insects can see movements that take place in as little as 1/1000 of a second.

- Caterpillars have more than 2,000 muscles in their tiny bodies.

- Some mosquitoes hunt by detecting their prey's body heat and homing in on it.

- Butterflies and moths are found in all places except Antarctica.

- Earwigs got their name from a myth that they crawl inside people's ears when they are sleeping! In truth, they never do.

- Leafcutter ants can lift and carry enormous weights. Some of their loads are equivalent to a young child carrying an 11-ton truck!

- When bees discover a good source of nectar, they tell other bees by doing a strange dance. But not all bees "speak" the same language—bees from one area cannot understand bees from other areas.

- A shocking 2.5 million people die each year in Africa from the bite of the malaria-carrying mosquito. This makes mosquitoes the most dangerous creatures alive.

- An adult dragonfly can see almost 360 degrees.

- Glowworms are not actually worms; they are beetles!

Insect quiz

The answers to these questions can all be found by looking back through the book. See how many you get right. You can check your answers on page 56.

1) How many legs does an insect have?
   A—four
   B—six
   C—eight

2) Butterflies and moths have wings covered in tiny . . .
   A—scales
   B—spots
   C—spikes

3) What do head lice eat?
   A—blood
   B—leaves
   C—skin

4) Which insect is good at weightlifting?
   A—leafhopper
   B—rhinoceros beetle
   C—ladybug

5) What makes an insect's wings so strong?
   A—veins
   B—muscles
   C—bones

6) What noise do some cockroaches make when they are disturbed?
   A—clicking
   B—squealing
   C—hissing

7) How do flies eat their food?
   A—by chopping it up
   B—by rolling it into a ball
   C—by turning it into a soupy mush

8) Which insect feeds on damp wood?
   A—deathwatch beetle
   B—grasshopper
   C—ladybug

9) What is the third stage of many insects' lives?
   A—egg
   B—adult
   C—pupa

10) Which insect young live underwater for their first year?
    A—dung beetles
    B—damselflies
    C—earwigs

11) Honeybees make honey from . . .
    A—flower nectar
    B—water
    C—mud

12) Which insect can walk on the surface of water?
    A—water strider
    B—dragonfly
    C—grasshopper

Find out more

Books to read

Beastly Bugs by Lynn Huggins Cooper,
   Franklin Watts, 2005
Classifying Animals: Insects by Sarah
   Wilkes, Hodder Wayland, 2007
From Egg to Adult: The Life Cycle of Insects
   by Richard and Louise Spilsbury,
   Heinemann Library, 2003
How Does It Grow: Butterfly by Jinny
   Johnson, Franklin Watts, 2009
*I Wonder Why Caterpillars Eat So Much:
   And Other Questions about Life Cycles*
   by Belinda Weber, Kingfisher, 2006
Weird Bugs by Kathryn Smith, Kingfisher,
   2010

Places to visit

Seattle Bug Safari, Seattle, Washington
www.seattlebugsafari.com
View an assortment of live insects,
spiders, scorpions, millipedes, and
centipedes. The organization also offers
traveling exhibitions as part of its
educational program.

Audubon Nature Institute, Insectarium,
New Orleans, Louisiana
www.auduboninstitute.org/visit/insectarium
View live and preserved insects specimens
at North America's largest museum
devoted to insects and their relatives,
including a garden featuring thousands
of free-flight butterflies.

Websites

www.yourdiscovery.com
A useful website for children and
teachers with a wide range of topics,
including insects.

http://kids.yahoo.com/animals/insects
Features facts and pictures of insects
ranging from the firefly to the stinkbug.

www.endangeredspecies.org
Learn about all of the endangered
insects in the world.

www.nhm.ac.uk
With a section just for children you will
find a picture gallery, games, and facts
about insects.

http://kids.nationalgeographic.com
Games, videos, stories, facts, and
activities on all science topics,
including insects.

Insect quiz answers

1) B	7) C
2) A	8) A
3) A	9) C
4) B	10) B
5) A	11) A
6) C	12) A